you are perfect

JUST THE WAY YOU ARE.

Meet Kitty, Puppy,
Bunny and Teddy.

Four best friends who could
not be more different.

Kitty loves unicorns
and dancing.

Puppy loves numbers
and reading.

Bunny loves trains and science.

Teddy loves dinosaurs and writing.

Kitty is great at sitting still
and listening to instructions.

Puppy can only listen if
he's moving his body.

Bunny remembers everything
that she hears.

Teddy can't always remember what he hears but remembers what he sees.

Sometimes Kitty gets upset
when things don't go the way
she planned.

Puppy loves trying new things and doesn't mind when plans get changed.

Bunny doesn't like strong smells or loud noises.

Teddy loves making noise and moving his body when he's happy.

Bunny and Teddy love big squeezes and tight hugs.

Puppy and kitty don't like it
if anyone gets too close to
their space.

Puppy and Bunny love playing together.

Kitty and Teddy would
rather play alone.

Kitty likes to talk **VERY LOUDLY** to everyone about everything.

Bunny likes to talk, but mostly about things she loves.

Teddy finds it easier to talk using pictures.

Puppy sometimes talks a lot and sometimes doesn't talk at all.

You see, Puppy, Kitty, Bunny and Teddy all see the world differently.

And that's ok, because there is no wrong way to see the world.

Sometimes the world around them can be a bit too much, and Puppy, Kitty, Bunny, and Teddy need time and space to themselves.

Sometimes they might get a little scared or sad, but that doesn't mean they don't want to be friends.

The best thing any friend can do is give space to friends who need it...and be there for friends who need them.

No matter how your brain sees the world and what you like or don't like, your unique experience is important and valid. You are perfect just the way you are.

Just like Puppy, Kitty,
Teddy and Bunny.

Four friends who are all different and deserving of happiness.

To find out more about how to help make spaces and places more inclusive for everyone, visit trueinclusion.ca

$1 from every sale of this book goes to support the True Inclusion Foundation of Canada.

Visit sarafurlongauthor.com for more children's book titles.

Made in the USA
Coppell, TX
19 February 2024

29203691R00021